Three Simple Rules for Christian Living
Leader Guide

Three Simple Rules

for Christian Living

A SIX-WEEK STUDY FOR ADULTS

LEADER GUIDE

ABINGDON PRESS
NASHVILLE

THREE SIMPLE RULES
FOR CHRISTIAN LIVING LEADER GUIDE:
A SIX-WEEK STUDY FOR ADULTS

This book is printed on elemental chlorine-free paper.

ISBN 978-1-5018-4017-3

08 09 10 11 12 13 14 15 16 17—10 9 8 7 6 5 4 3 2 1
MANUFACTURED IN THE UNITED STATES OF AMERICA

CONTENTS

INTRODUCTION

Three Simple Rules for Christian Living Leader Guide provides extended reflection on three principles of Christian living illuminated by John Wesley in the General Rules and revisited by Bishop Rueben Job in his book *Three Simple Rules: A Wesleyan Way of Living*: do no harm, do good, and stay in love with God. This study is designed to help you return to those early Wesleyan understandings of spiritual disciplines that can transform us and the world in which we live. As you take this journey of reflection and practice, you will discover that these three rules can lead you to a more faithful way of living as a disciple of Jesus Christ.

In this six-session study, you will explore the study book, *Three Simple Rules for Christian Living*, and view excerpts from conversations with Rueben Job in order to learn more about the three rules and how to practice them in daily life. Each rule has a session to help you understand the rule and a session to help you explore ways to practice the rule. Through the words of John Wesley, Rueben Job, and the Bible, you will reflect on what these rules meant during Wesley's time and what they can mean to us today. You will also identify ways the practice of these rules can change your daily life and the lives of those around you.

Your church can do a church-wide study of the three simple rules by using the youth resource, *Three Simple Rules 24/7*, and the children's resource, *Three Simple Rules for Following Jesus*, along with the adult study book, *Three Simple Rules for Christian Living*.

RESOURCE COMPONENTS

The resources and group sessions in this study function together to engage learners with spiritual practices associated with the three simple rules of Christian life: do no harm, do good, and stay in love with God. It is based on the book *Three Simple Rules*, by Rueben Job. The resources include a study book for each participant, a DVD for the group, and this leader guide.

- **The Study Book,** *Three Simple Rules for Christian Living*, is designed to facilitate the understanding and practice of the three rules. It can be used for both individual and group study. Each person in a group should have his or her own copy. The book contains the main content of the study and space for writing responses to key reflection questions about understanding and practicing the three simple rules.
- **The DVD** contains 5-6-minute excerpts from interviews with Bishop Rueben Job.
- **The Leader Guide** provides all a leader needs to facilitate a *Three Simple Rules for Christian Living* group study.

Study Book Features

Three Simple Rules for Christian Living is designed to help the reader understand and practice the three simple rules of living a Christian life. This is accomplished through the content of the study book and with several specific features in each chapter.

- **Focus Questions:** Each chapter begins with focus questions that engage the learner more deeply with what the rule means and how it can be practiced in daily life. Learners will respond to the questions as they read the content. They will discuss their responses during the session.
- **Prayer:** Each chapter begins with a brief prayer that is closely related to the focus question.
- **Learners** will spend six weeks studying the three simple rules. Two chapters, a chapter on concept and a chapter on application, guide the study of each of the rules. The concept chapter, "Understanding the Rule," will help learners reflect on what the rule means. The application chapter, "Practicing the Rule," will help learners explore ways to apply the rule in daily life.
- **The main content** of the chapters is divided into two main sections: "What Does the Rule Say?" and "What Does the Bible Say?"
- **The study book** is designed so that learners can write responses in their books. "Reflect on the Rule" activities will engage them more deeply with the rules. "Reflect on the Bible" activities will help them make connections between the Bible and the rule. "Reflect" activities will facilitate engagement with the actual content of the chapter.
- **Every chapter** concludes with "A Guide for Daily Prayer" that is based on the model in Rueben Job's book *Three Simple Rules*. Learners are encouraged to use the guide for personal prayer between the sessions.

DVD Features

- **The 5-6-minute segments** from an interview with Rueben Job are intended to inspire and motivate the learner to want to know more about the rules and how to practice them in daily life.
- **Each session** includes viewing a DVD segment followed by questions for reflecting on the video content.

Leader Guide Features

- **Step-by-step instructions** for leading the sessions, including questions and activities based on the study book and the DVD segments.
- **Intergenerational worship ideas** that include group activities for adults, youth, and children.
- **A Guide for Daily Prayer**, including Welcoming God's Presence, Scripture, Meditation, Prayer, and Blessing.

HOW TO ORGANIZE A GROUP

Follow these basic steps for the best results in starting a group for *Three Simple Rules for Christian Living*.

- **Read** through the study book and any Bible readings mentioned in the chapters. Obtain a copy of *Three Simple Rules* by Rueben Job, and read it. View the interview excerpts on the DVD. Review instructions in the leader guide. Think about the rules dealt with in the study and any issues they generate. Prepare to respond to questions that someone may ask about the study.
- **Develop** a list of potential participants. An ideal size for a small group is seven to twelve people. Your list should have about twice your target number (fourteen to twenty-four people). Encourage your local church to purchase a copy of *Three Simple Rules for Christian Living* and a copy of Rueben Job's book *Three Simple Rules* for each of the people on your list. This is an invaluable outreach tool.
- **Decide** on a location and time for your group.
- **Identify** someone who is willing to go with you to visit the people on your list. Make it your goal to become acquainted with each person you visit. Tell them about *Three Simple Rules for Christian Living*. Give them a copy of the study book that you will be using for your group and a copy of Rueben Job's book *Three Simple Rules*.

Encourage them to read the book and respond to the questions. Even if those you visit choose not to attend the group at this time, they will have an opportunity to study the books on their own. Tell each person the initial meeting time, location, and how many weeks the group will meet. Invite them to become a part of the group. Thank them for their time.

- **Publicize** the study through as many channels as are available through your local church and your community.
- **A few days before** the sessions begin, give a friendly phone call or send an e-mail to thank all persons you visited for their consideration and interest. Remind them of the time and location of the first meeting.

HOW TO LEAD A GROUP

The role of the leader is to prepare for and facilitate the group sessions in order to help people understand the three simple rules for Christian living and apply them to their lives. A leader is not expected to be an expert. In fact, a leader often learns along with the participants. So what does a leader do?

A Leader Prepares

This leader guide contains specific instructions for planning and implementing the study, *Three Simple Rules for Christian Living*. Generally speaking, however, a leader has some basic preparation responsibilities. They are:

Pray

Ask for God's guidance as you prepare to lead the session.

Read and Reflect

Review the session chapter, the leader guide session plan, and the DVD segment ahead of time. Jot down questions or insights that occur during your review.

Think About Group Participants

Who are they? What life issues do they have? What questions might they have about the chapter and its featured rule for Christian living?

Prepare the Learning Area

Gather any needed supplies, such as large sheets of paper, markers, paper and pencils, Bibles, audiovisual equipment, masking tape, Bible dictionaries and commentaries, and supplies needed for the worship experiences. Make sure everyone will have a place to sit.

Pray for the Group Participants

Before the participants arrive, pray for each one. Ask for God's blessing on your session. Offer thanks to God for the opportunity to lead the session.

A Leader Creates a Welcoming Atmosphere

Hospitality is a spiritual discipline. A leader helps to create an environment that makes others feel welcome and helps every participant experience the freedom to ask questions and to state opinions. Such an atmosphere is based upon mutual respect.

Greet Participants as They Arrive

As participants arrive, welcome them to the study. If participants are not familiar with one another, provide nametags and make introductions.

Listen

As group discussion unfolds, affirm the comments and ideas of participants. Avoid the temptation to dominate conversation or "correct" the ideas of participants.

Affirm

Thank people for talking about what they think or feel. Acknowledge their contributions to discussion in positive ways, even if you disagree with their ideas.

A Leader Facilitates Discussion

Ask Questions

Use the questions suggested in the session plans or other questions that occur to you as you prepare for the session. Encourage others to ask questions.

Invite Silent Participants to Contribute Ideas

If someone in the group is quiet, you might say something like, "I'm interested in what you're thinking." If participants seem hesitant or shy, do not pressure them to speak. However, do communicate your interest.

When Someone in the Group Dominates

You can handle this in several ways. Remind the group as a whole that everyone's ideas are important. Invite them to respect one another and to allow others the opportunity to express their ideas. You may establish a group covenant that clarifies such mutual respect. Use structured methods such as going around the circle to allow everyone a chance to speak. Only as a last resort, speak to the person who dominates conversation after the group meeting.

A PLAN FOR GROUP STUDY

As you lead your group through the study book, *Three Simple Rules for Christian Living*, you will move through a regular sequence of activities described in the following paragraphs. These activities are designed to bring the group together, to create an environment for learning and faith development, and to help the group explore the three simple rules for Christian living and how to practice them in everyday life. The aim is for all who participate in the study to become confident in understanding and practicing the rules and to grow in faith and commitment to Jesus Christ. Details of how to prepare for and implement discussion, week by week, are spelled out in this leader guide under "Session Plans."

Prepare Ahead

Review the chapter, the DVD segments, and the Session Plans. Gather supplies and set up the learning area. Create a worship center according to the instructions in the Session Plans.

Welcome the Participants

Greet participants, especially members who are new to the study. Invite them to use nametags and make them feel welcome.

Consider the Rule

Each chapter of the study book, *Three Simple Rules for Christian Living*, focuses on one of the three simple rules for Christian life. Read the Focus Question about the rule and allow time for response to the question.

Pray Together

Each chapter in the study book begins with a brief prayer. Pray the printed prayer aloud. You can also invite the entire group to read the printed prayer aloud. You may also choose to pray your own prayer. Do what seems appropriate for your group.

View the DVD Segment

Each session includes a 5-6-minute excerpt from an interview with Bishop Rueben Job that relates to the rule for the session. Show the DVD segment and ask the questions in the leader guide to stimulate discussion about it.

Reflect and Respond

Each chapter has two major sections: "What Does the Rule Say?" and "What Does the Bible Say?" In the section entitled "What Does the Rule Say?" you will find an activity entitled "Reflect on the Rule." Participants will respond to the questions in this activity in order to assess their own awareness of what the rule means and how they can practice it. In the section entitled "What Does the Bible Say?" you will find an activity entitled "Reflect on the Bible." Participants will read the Bible passage and respond to questions about how it informs the rule and its practice. In addition, you will find general reflection questions in the activity entitled "Reflect." These questions are about the chapter content and are located near the information to which they refer. Allow time for discussion, dialogue, and questions from everyone in the group. Encourage participants to read the chapters and respond to the questions before they come to the group session.

Close the Session

Each of the sessions closes with a guide for daily prayer based upon the model in Rueben Job's book *Three Simple Rules*. Use this guide as a way to pray and reflect on the rule featured in the chapter. Encourage the group to use the guide for personal daily prayer between the sessions as they incorporate the rule into their daily lives.

SESSION PLANS

CHAPTER 1

DO NO HARM –
Understanding the Rule

PREPARE AHEAD

Set Up the Learning Area

- Prepare a worship center. Find a small table and cover with an attractive cloth. Place a candle in a candleholder, and place it on the table. Have matches nearby. Place a Bible on the table. Make a poster that lists the three rules: Do No Harm, Do Good, Stay in Love With God. Place this poster where all can see it.
- Prepare a graffiti sheet by writing the words "Do No Harm – Understanding the Rule" at the top of a large white sheet of paper or poster board. Put this graffiti sheet where participants can easily write on it—a wall or a tabletop, for example.
- Arrange chairs in a circle or around a table. Make sure everyone will have a place to sit. Be sensitive to the needs of persons who have disabilities.

Gather Needed Materials

- A copy of *Three Simple Rules for Christian Living* for each participant in the group
- The DVD for *Three Simple Rules for Christian Living*
- This leader guide, in order to have the session plan easily available for your use.
- (Optional) A copy or copies of Rueben Job's book *Three Simple Rules*
- (Optional) *The Book of Discipline of The United Methodist Church* (The United Methodist Publishing House, 2004)
- Bibles. If possible, provide several different translations or paraphrases such as the Common English Bible, the New King James Version, the New Revised Standard Version, and *THE MESSAGE.*
- Bible dictionaries and commentaries
- Paper, markers, paper, pencils, nametags
- Whiteboard or newsprint and markers
- Audiovisual equipment: a DVD player and TV for showing the DVD segment for this session

WELCOME THE PARTICIPANTS

Greet the participants as they arrive. Show them the worship center and where additional Bibles and Bible resources are located. If they do not already have a study book, give them one. Invite them to write or draw on the graffiti sheet "Do No Harm – Understanding the Rule" any ideas or images that define what the rule means. Tell them to create a nametag and to find a place to sit.

INTRODUCE THE STUDY

Tell the group that *Three Simple Rules for Christian Living* is based on John Wesley's three rules for living a Christian life, which are featured in the book *Three Simple Rules* by Bishop Rueben Job. Summarize the information about the rules in the Introduction of the study book. If you have a copy of *The Book of Discipline of The United Methodist Church*, show them the section entitled, "The Nature, Design, and General Rules of Our United Societies" in Paragraph 103.

CONSIDER THE QUESTIONS

Invite someone to read aloud the focus question for the rule: Most Christians do not intend to harm anyone; however, we sometimes are not aware of the harm we do. What does it mean to "do no harm"? Invite them to write responses in the space provided in their books. Discuss their responses. Look at the graffiti sheet responses. Invite participants to tell about what they have written or drawn.

PRAY TOGETHER

Invite the group to pray aloud the prayer that is printed in their books: God of love, we know you want us to love your creation: neighbors, friends or enemies, strangers, the natural world, and ourselves. Yet we do harm, often unintentionally. Help us to be more aware of the harm we do. In Christ we pray. Amen.

VIEW THE DVD SEGMENT

Show the DVD segment for session 1 "Do No Harm – Understanding the Rule." Invite participants to respond to the following questions:

1. How would you respond differently to people if you knew they would always follow the rule "Do no harm"?
2. Rueben Job states that we cannot practice this rule without trust in God. What do you think he means? Do you agree?

3. Why are the Beatitudes so helpful regarding this rule? What do we
    learn from them about doing no harm?

REFLECT AND RESPOND

What Does the Rule Say?

- Have participants write responses to the questions in "Reflect
  on the Rule." Where is harm being done? (Use an example
  from your household or circle of friends, your family, your
  congregation, your community, your city, your state, a group
  of people with whom you identify, your nation, or the world.)
  Who is being harmed? What harm is being done? Who is
  doing it or causing it? (The "who" may be one or more people,
  groups, corporations, institutions, states, or nations.) Why is it
  happening? How is harm being done? Invite them to tell about
  their responses.
- Read or tell in your own words the remaining information
  in "Unintended Harm." Invite participants to respond to
  the questions in "Reflect." How do you respond to Job's
  understanding that the rule "do no harm" can provide a safe
  place to stand during the work of discernment? Why do you
  think the rule requires radical trust and obedience in God?
  Discuss their responses.
- Read or tell in your own words the information in "John Wesley's
  General Rules." Invite participants to respond to the question in
  "Reflect." If you were writing John Wesley's General Rules for
  doing no harm today, what would you put on the list? Discuss
  their responses.
- Read or tell in your own words the information in the opening
  paragraph of "The Answers Depend on the Questions." Invite
  participants to respond to the questions in "Reflect." How do
  the questions in this paragraph affect your awareness of harm

caused by groups or institutions? How might you unwittingly be part of the group? Discuss their responses. Read or tell in your own words the remaining information in this section. Have participants respond to the questions in "Reflect." If you see yourself as part of the group or institution that might be causing harm, what changes could you make? How might you influence change in the group or institution to make changes that would reduce the harm being done? Discuss their responses.

What Does the Bible Say?

- Read or tell in your own words the information about preparing to get a driver's license in the opening paragraph. Invite participants to tell about their memories of getting a license.
- Have participants open their Bibles to Exodus 20:1-17. Read the Ten Commandments aloud or silently. Invite participants to write responses to the question in "Reflect on the Bible." What connections do you see between the Ten Commandments and the rule to do no harm? Have them tell about their responses.
- Read or tell in your own words the remaining information in this section. Invite participants to respond to the questions in "Reflect." Which of the commandments concern doing no harm? In each, what kind of harm is prohibited? Who is being protected from harm? Do any of these commandments also protect the one who might do harm? If so, how? Discuss their responses.
- Read or tell in your own words the information in "Ultimate Loyalty." Invite participants to respond to the questions in "Reflect." What are your ultimate loyalties? What might your checkbook or credit card statement tell you about what you value most? To what goals do you give your greatest efforts? What does your lifestyle tell you and other people about your values? Are your ultimate loyalties doing harm to what God loves: the earth and all of creation, including human creatures? Discuss their responses.

CLOSE THE SESSION

- Invite the group to use "Closing – A Guide for Daily Prayer" during the week ahead for their personal prayer. Tell them to read Chapter 2, "Do No Harm – Practicing the Rule" and to write responses in the reflection activities.

- Pray aloud the prayer in "Welcoming God's Presence." *Gracious God, open our eyes to love what you love so that we will do no harm. Uphold and guide us during this season of Lent as we seek to follow your commandments and abide in your ways. Amen.*

- Read aloud Psalm 19:7-8, 12-13a, which is printed in "Scripture."

- Tell participants to write about insights, words, or ideas that come to them as they reflect on Psalm 19:7-8, 12-13a according to the instructions in "Meditation." After a few moments, read aloud Psalm 19:14.

- Invite the group to pray according to the instructions in "Prayer." They may pray aloud or silently. Close the time of prayer by saying aloud "Amen."

- Read aloud Isaiah 30:15b in "Blessing" as a dismissal for the session.

CHAPTER

DO NO HARM –
Practicing the Rule

PREPARE AHEAD

Set Up the Learning Area

- Prepare a worship center. Find a small table and cover with an attractive cloth. Place a candle in a candleholder, and place it on the table. Have matches nearby. Place a Bible on the table. Make a poster that lists the three rules: Do No Harm, Do Good, Stay in Love With God. Place this poster where all can see it.
- Prepare a graffiti sheet by writing the words "Do No Harm – Practicing the Rule" at the top of a large white sheet of paper or poster board. Put this graffiti sheet in a place such as a wall or a tabletop where participants can easily write on it.
- Arrange chairs in a circle or around a table. Make sure everyone will have a place to sit. Be sensitive to the needs of persons who have disabilities.

Gather Needed Materials

- A copy of *Three Simple Rules for Christian Living* for each participant in the group
- The DVD for *Three Simple Rules for Christian Living*
- This leader guide, in order to have the session plan easily available for your use.
- (Optional) A copy or copies of Rueben Job's book *Three Simple Rules*
- Bibles. If possible, provide several different translations or paraphrases such as the Common English Bible, the New King James Version, the New Revised Standard Version, and *THE MESSAGE.*
- Bible dictionaries and commentaries
- Paper, markers, paper, pencils, nametags
- Whiteboard or newsprint and markers
- Audiovisual equipment: a DVD player and TV for showing the DVD segment for this session

WELCOME THE PARTICIPANTS

Greet the participants as they arrive. Show them the worship center and where additional Bibles and Bible resources are located. If they do not already have a study book, give them one. Invite them to write or draw on the graffiti sheet "Do No Harm – Practicing the Rule" any ideas or images they have about practicing the rule. Tell them to create a nametag and to find a place to sit.

CONSIDER THE QUESTIONS

Invite someone to read aloud the focus question for the rule. How can we put into practice the rule of doing no harm? What difference can our practice make in our own lives and in the lives of others? Invite them to write responses in the space provided in their books. Discuss their responses. Look at the graffiti sheet response. Invite participants to tell about what they have written or drawn.

PRAY TOGETHER

Invite the group to pray aloud the prayer that is printed in their books: God of love and grace, when our anger, indignation, indifference, or greed cause us to want to do harm, give us strength and courage to resist. When we think you are asking the impossible of us, give us the mindfulness and strength to do no harm. Amen.

VIEW THE DVD SEGMENT

Show the DVD segment for session 2, "Do No Harm – Practicing the Rule." Invite participants to respond to the following questions:

1. If your congregation tried seriously to practice this rule, what changes might occur?
2. How might your home be different if family members practiced this rule?
3. In discussing this rule, Rueben Job talks about creating a "safe place" and a "level playing field." What do you think he means?

REFLECT AND RESPOND

What Does the Rule Say?

- Read the section entitled "What Would You Never Do?"
- Have participants write responses to the questions in "Reflect on the Rule." Within the realm of real possibility what would you

never do? What connections do you see between this question and practicing the rule to do no harm? What are some other ways you might practice this rule? What are some ways your church, business, school, or some other institution might practice this rule? Invite them to tell about their responses.

- Read or tell in your own words the information in "Intentionally Doing No Harm." Invite participants to respond to the questions in "Reflect." How do you respond to Job's statement that we "stand on common ground, inhabit a common and precious space, share a common faith, feast at a common table, and have an equal measure of God's unlimited love"? How might this understanding change your view of those with whom you disagree? Discuss their responses.
- Read or tell in your own words the information in "Collective Harm." Invite participants to respond to the questions in "Reflect." What would you add to list of who or what is being harmed in the 21st century? What practices do you think would alleviate the harm? How might you be part of the solution? Discuss their responses.

What Does the Bible Say?

- Read the opening sentence in the section "Romans 14:14-23."
- Have participants open their Bibles to Romans 14:14-23. Read aloud or silently. Invite participants to write responses to the question in "Reflect on the Bible." What connections do you see between this Bible passage and the intentional practice of doing no harm? Have them tell about their responses.
- Read or tell in your own words the remaining information in this section. Invite participants to respond to the questions in "Reflect." How would you translate to people in the 21st century Paul's concern about not causing our brother or sister to stumble? When have you refrained from doing something that

you considered perfectly ethical in order to do no harm to your sisters and brothers? Discuss their responses.

- Read the section entitled "Matthew 5:38-48."
- Have participants open their Bibles to Matthew 5:38-48. Read the Bible passage aloud or silently. Invite participants to write responses to the questions in "Reflect on the Bible." What challenges you in this Bible reading? How does it relate to the practice of doing no harm? Have them tell about their responses.
- Tell in your own words the information in "Jesus' Third Way." Invite participants to respond to the questions in "Reflect." How do you respond to Walter Wink's interpretation of the difficult passages in Matthew 5? What challenges you or makes you curious? Do you agree or disagree with his interpretations? Why? Discuss their responses.
- Read or tell in your own words the information in "Retaliation or Not?" Invite participants to respond to the questions in "Reflect." Recall times when you have not retaliated. What were your motives for not seeking revenge? In these times were you able to preserve your own dignity and self-respect? Can you anticipate some situations in the near future when you may be tempted to retaliate? Discuss their responses.

CLOSE THE SESSION

- Invite the group to use "Closing – A Guide for Daily Prayer" during the week ahead for their personal prayer. Tell them to read Chapter 3, "Do Good – Understanding the Rule" and to write responses in the reflection activities.
- Pray aloud the prayer in "Welcoming God's Presence." *God of justice and mercy, you want us to love our enemies and to do them no harm. Forgive us when we fail, and help us to practice that kind of love. Amen.*

- Read aloud Psalm 1:1-2, which is printed in "Scripture." Tell participants to write about insights, words, or ideas that come to them as they reflect on Psalm 1:1-2 according to the instructions in "Meditation."
- Invite the group to pray according to the instructions in "Prayer." They may pray aloud or silently. Close the time of prayer by saying aloud "Amen."
- Read aloud Psalm 1:3a in "Blessing" as a dismissal for the session.

CHAPTER 3

DO GOOD –
Understanding the Rule

PREPARE AHEAD

Set Up the Learning Area

- Prepare a worship center. Find a small table and cover with an attractive cloth. Place a candle in a candleholder, and place it on the table. Have matches nearby. Place a Bible on the table. Make a poster that lists the three rules: Do No Harm, Do Good, Stay in Love With God. Place this poster where all can see it.
- Prepare a graffiti sheet by writing the words "Do Good – Understanding the Rule" at the top of a large white sheet of paper or poster board. Put this graffiti sheet in a place such as a wall or a tabletop where participants can easily write on it.
- Arrange chairs in a circle or around a table. Make sure everyone will have a place to sit. Be sensitive to the needs of persons who have disabilities.

Gather Needed Materials

- A copy of *Three Simple Rules for Christian Living* for each participant in the group
- The DVD for *Three Simple Rules for Christian Living*
- This leader guide, in order to have the session plan easily available for your use.
- (Optional) A copy or copies of Rueben Job's book *Three Simple Rules*
- Bibles. If possible, provide several different translations or paraphrases such as the Common English Bible, the New King James Version, the New Revised Standard Version, and *THE MESSAGE*.
- Bible dictionaries and commentaries
- Paper, markers, paper, pencils, nametags
- Whiteboard or newsprint and markers
- Audiovisual equipment: a DVD player and TV for showing the DVD segment for this session

WELCOME THE PARTICIPANTS

Greet the participants as they arrive. Show them the worship center and where additional Bibles and Bible resources are located. Invite them to write or draw on the graffiti sheet "Do Good – Understanding the Rule" any ideas or images that define what the rule means. Tell them to create a nametag and to find a place to sit.

CONSIDER THE QUESTIONS

Invite someone to read aloud the focus question for the rule. Most of us think of ourselves as good people. What does it mean to do good? Invite them to write responses in the space provided in their study books. Discuss

their responses. Look at the graffiti sheet responses. Invite participa
tell about what they have written or drawn.

PRAY TOGETHER

Invite the group to pray aloud the prayer that is printed in their study books: Holy God, open our eyes that we may see what good needs doing; open our imaginations that we may figure out what good we can do; and open our hearts to your empowering love that we may have the courage to act. Through Christ we pray. Amen.

VIEW THE DVD SEGMENT

Show the DVD segment for session 3, "Do Good – Understanding the Rule." Invite participants to respond to the following questions:

1. Think of times in your own life when you "did good" to an enemy. What was the result?
2. Think of times when your good deeds were rejected? How did it feel? What did you learn?
3. Rueben Job says that doing good can sometimes "get out of hand." What do you think he means?

REFLECT AND RESPOND

What Does the Rule Say?

- Read the section entitled "Bread or No Bread."
- Have participants write responses to the instructions and questions in "Reflect on the Rule." Quickly jot down a list of ten ways to do good. Then reflect on your list. What do these ten

ways tell you about what "doing good" means to you? Which of these ways involve you as the actor? Which involve you along with other people? Which do not involve you at all? Invite them to tell about their responses.

- Read or tell in your own words the information in "Seeing the Need." Invite participants to respond to the questions in "Reflect." What do you really need? Which of your needs could you really do without? What does the marketplace tell you about what you need? Does the world of advertising and consumerism ever address what the community needs? Who or what is looking out for the common good? Discuss their responses.

- Read or tell in your own words the information in "Your Deep Gladness and the World's Deep Hunger." Invite participants to respond to the questions in "Reflect." What are your talents? What gives you a sense of deep gladness? What needs in your community might benefit from them?

- Read or tell in your own words the remaining information in this section. Invite participants to respond to the questions in "Reflect." How do you respond to Wesley's ideas about doing good and helping the poor? What challenges you? Why? What appeals to you? Why? Discuss their responses.

- Read or tell in your own words the information in "Doing Good and God's Grace." Invite participants to respond to the questions in "Reflect." What connections do you see between doing good and God's grace? Discuss their responses.

What Does the Bible Say?

- Invite participants to write responses in "Reflect on the Bible." How do the following Bible passages help you define what it means to do good? Exodus 20:12-17; Leviticus 19:18; The Great Commandment in Matthew 22:37-40; Mark 12:28-33; and Luke 10:27; Micah 6:6-8; James 1:19-27; 2:14-17. Discuss their responses.

- Read or tell in your own words the information in "What Does the Bible Say?" Invite participants to respond to the questions in "Reflect." In your experience, how does faith lead to works? How has your faith led you to do good? Discuss their responses.

CLOSE THE SESSION

- Invite the group to use "Closing – A Guide for Daily Prayer" during the week ahead for their personal prayer. Tell them to read Chapter 4, "Do Good – Practicing the Rule" and to write responses in the reflection activities.
- Pray aloud the prayer in "Welcoming God's Presence." *God of love and grace, help us to see our neighbors' needs and to respond in acts of love and mercy. In Christ's name we pray. Amen.*
- Read aloud Ephesians 2:8-10, which is printed in "Scripture."
- Tell participants to write about insights, words, or ideas that come to them as they reflect on Ephesians 2:8-10 according to the instructions in "Meditation."
- Invite the group to pray according to the instructions in "Prayer." They may pray aloud or silently. Close the time of prayer by saying aloud "Amen."
- Read aloud Psalm 106:3 in the section entitled "Blessing" as a dismissal for the session.

DO GOOD –
Practicing the Rule

PREPARE AHEAD

Set Up the Learning Area

- Prepare a worship center. Find a small table and cover with an attractive cloth. Place a candle in a candleholder, and place it on the table. Have matches nearby. Place a Bible on the table. Make a poster that lists the three rules: Do No Harm, Do Good, Stay in Love With God. Place this poster where all can see it.
- Prepare a graffiti sheet by writing the words "Do Good – Practicing the Rule" at the top of a large white sheet of paper or poster board. Put this graffiti sheet in a place such as a wall or a tabletop where participants can easily write on it.
- Arrange chairs in a circle or around a table. Make sure everyone will have a place to sit. Be sensitive to the needs of persons who have disabilities.

Gather Needed Materials

- A copy of *Three Simple Rules for Christian Living* for each participant in the group
- The DVD for *Three Simple Rules for Christian Living*
- This leader guide, in order to have the session plan easily available for your use.
- (Optional) A copy or copies of Rueben Job's book *Three Simple Rules*
- Bibles. If possible, provide several different translations or paraphrases such as the Common English Bible, the New King James Version, the New Revised Standard Version, and *THE MESSAGE*.
- Bible dictionaries and commentaries
- Paper, markers, paper, pencils, nametags
- Whiteboard or newsprint and markers
- Audiovisual equipment: a DVD player and TV for showing the DVD segment for this session

WELCOME THE PARTICIPANTS

Greet the participants as they arrive. Show them the worship center and where additional Bibles and Bible resources are located. Invite them to write or draw on the graffiti sheet "Do Good – Practicing the Rule" any ideas or images they have about practicing the rule. Tell them to create a nametag and to find a place to sit.

CONSIDER THE QUESTIONS

Invite someone to read aloud the focus question for the rule. How can we put into practice the rule of doing good? What difference can our actions make in our own lives and in the lives of others? Invite participants to write responses in the space provided in their study books. Discuss their responses. Look at the graffiti sheet response. Invite participants to tell about what they have written or drawn.

PRAY TOGETHER

Invite the group to pray aloud the prayer that is printed in their study books: Everlasting God, as we put into practice this rule of doing good, show us the way past our doubts and fears, and give us confidence and resolve to make a difference. In Christ's name. Amen.

VIEW THE DVD SEGMENT

Show the DVD segment for session 4, "Do Good – Practicing the Rule." Invite participants to respond to the following questions:

1. What are some examples of healthy self-denial? of unhealthy self-denial?
2. How do you think your life might be different if you truly believed that the image of God was "fresh stamped on your heart"?
3. What are some ways that you could practice doing good among your family or friends?

REFLECT AND RESPOND

What Does the Rule Say?

- Read or tell in your own words the opening paragraph in "What Does the Rule Say?"
- Have participants respond to the questions in "Reflect on the Rule." What are some ways you have practiced the rule to do good? What challenges have you identified in your efforts to practice this rule? Invite them to tell about their responses.

- Read or tell in your own words the story in "Anathoth Community Garden." Invite participants to respond to the questions in "Reflect." What potential positive effects for good do you see in the story of the Anathoth Community Garden? What are some of the unseen benefits to the community? What potential exists in your community for a community garden? Invite them to tell about their responses.

- Read the opening paragraph in "The Fear of Doing Good." Have participants respond to the question in "Reflect." What questions would you add to the list of fears? Invite them to tell about their responses.

- Read or tell in your own words the story of Amanda Block and Street Sheets in "The Fear of Doing Good." Have participants respond to the questions in "Reflect." How do you respond to the story of Amanda Block and Street Sheets? Have you ever seen the opportunity to do good but were overwhelmed with the extent of need? How did you respond? If you were able to go forward with your efforts, what empowered you? Invite participants to tell about their responses.

- Read or tell in your own words the paragraphs about the possibility of being rejected or ridiculed for doing good. Have participants respond to the questions in "Reflect." Have there been times you have retreated from doing good because of fear of rejection and ridicule? Can you recall times when you chose to do good in the face of rejection? If so, what empowered you? Invite them to tell about their responses.

What Does the Bible Say?

- Read aloud the opening sentence in "What Does the Bible Say?" Invite participants to read the Bible passages and respond to the instructions in "Reflect on the Bible." Prayerfully read the following Scriptures and write notes about the ways they speak to you about the practice of doing good. How do they inspire you

to practice doing good? 1 John 3:17-18; Romans 12; G
5:22–6:2. Invite them to tell about their responses. If yo
time, you may choose to have the group form three teams. Assign
one of the above Bible readings to each team. Have them read their
assigned Scripture and discuss it in the team. Share highlights of
the team discussions with the entire group.

- Read or tell in your own words the information in the section
  entitled "1 John 3:17-18." Invite participants to respond to the
  questions in "Reflect." Would your congregation never ignore a
  brother or sister's basic need? Would they put their commitment
  in writing? Would you personally make that kind of commitment?
  Discuss their responses.

- Read or tell in your own words the information in the section
  entitled "Romans 12." Invite participants to respond to the
  questions in "Reflect." What gifts do you see in the people of your
  church community? How are these gifts used to practice doing
  good? How can you use your gifts for the practice of doing good?
  How do you think the community outside your church is affected
  by using your gifts to do good? Discuss their responses.

- Read or tell in your own words the information in the section
  entitled "Galatians 5:22–6:2." Invite participants to respond to the
  questions in "Reflect." How has your Christian community been
  shaped by grace? How has grace transformed the deeds of the
  community? How has grace shaped your community's efforts to
  do good in the larger society? Discuss their responses.

CLOSE THE SESSION

- Invite the group to use "Closing – A Guide for Daily Prayer"
  during the week ahead for their personal prayer. Tell them to read
  Chapter 5, "Stay in Love With God – Understanding the Rule" and
  to write responses in the reflection activities.

- Pray aloud the prayer in "Welcoming God's Presence."
  God of gentleness and love, through the ages you have empowered

your people to do good. In a world which overwhelms us with opportunities to do good, show us how to make a difference. In Christ's name we pray. Amen.

- Read aloud Romans 12:14-18, which is printed in "Scripture."
- Tell participants to write about insights, words, or ideas that come to them as they reflect on Romans 12:14-18 according to the instructions in "Meditation."
- Invite the group to pray according to the instructions in "Prayer." They may pray aloud or silently. Close the time of prayer by saying aloud "Amen."
- Read aloud the words in "Blessing" as a dismissal for the session.

STAY IN LOVE WITH GOD –
Understanding the Rule

PREPARE AHEAD

Set Up the Learning Area

- Prepare a worship center. Find a small table and cover with an attractive cloth. Place a candle in a candleholder, and place it on the table. Have matches nearby. Place a Bible on the table. Make a poster that lists the three rules: Do No Harm, Do Good, Stay in Love With God. Place this poster where all can see it.
- Prepare a graffiti sheet by writing the words "Stay in Love With God – Understanding the Rule" at the top of a large white sheet of paper or poster board. Put this graffiti sheet in a place such as a wall or a tabletop where participants can easily write on it.

- Arrange chairs in a circle or around a table. Make sure everyone will have a place to sit. Be sensitive to the needs of persons who have disabilities.

Gather Needed Materials

- A copy of *Three Simple Rules for Christian Living* for each participant in the group
- The DVD for *Three Simple Rules for Christian Living*
- This leader guide, in order to have the session plan easily available for your use.
- (Optional) A copy or copies of Rueben Job's book *Three Simple Rules*
- Bibles. If possible, provide several different translations or paraphrases such as the Common English Bible, the New King James Version, the New Revised Standard Version, and *THE MESSAGE*.
- Bible dictionaries and commentaries
- Paper, markers, paper, pencils, nametags
- Whiteboard or newsprint and markers
- Audiovisual equipment: a DVD player and TV for showing the DVD segment for this session

WELCOME THE PARTICIPANTS

Greet the participants as they arrive. Show them the worship center and where additional Bibles and Bible resources are located. Invite them to write or draw on the graffiti sheet "Stay in Love With God – Understanding the Rule" any ideas or images that define what the rule means. Tell them to create a nametag and to find a place to sit.

CONSIDER THE QUESTIONS

Invite someone to read aloud the focus question for the rule. Christians love God. What does it mean to stay in love with God? Invite them to

write responses in the space provided in their study books. D
responses. Look at the graffiti sheet response. Invite participa
about what they have written or drawn.

PRAY TOGETHER

Invite the group to pray aloud the prayer that is printed in their books: O God, the source of our being, we know you love us, and yet we don't always do our part to stay in touch. Help us to be formed in the disciplines that will keep us in loving relationship with you. In Christ's name. Amen.

VIEW THE DVD SEGMENT

Show the DVD segment for session 5, "Stay in Love With God – Understanding the Rule." Invite participants to respond to the following questions:

1. What are some ways that you try to "stay in love with God"?
2. In what ways does this rule help support and make possible our keeping the other two rules?
3. What are some ways that you've caught yourself trying to be God? What were the results?

REFLECT AND RESPOND

What Does the Rule Say?

- Read the opening sentence in this section. Have participants respond to the questions in "Reflect on the Rule." What is your initial impression of the rule to stay in love with God? What images or ideas come to your mind when you hear this rule? Discuss their responses.

45

- Read or tell in your own words the information in "Life Disciplines." Have participants write responses to the questions in "Reflect." What disciplines are you currently observing in your own life? What disciplines have you observed in the past? What challenges or benefits resulted from these disciplines? Discuss their responses.

- Read or tell in your own words the information in "Spiritual Disciplines as Means of Grace." Have participants write responses to the questions in "Reflect." Which discipline or "means of grace" appeals most to you? Why? How do you respond to the idea that consistent practice of these disciplines keeps us in touch with Christ's presence and power? Discuss their responses.

- Read or tell in your own words the information in "Prayer." Have participants write responses to the questions in "Reflect." How do you respond to Wesley's discipline for personal and public prayer? Does it appeal to you? Why or why not? Discuss their responses.

- Read or tell in your own words the information in "Worship and the Lord's Supper." Have participants write responses to the questions in "Reflect." What is your experience of the Lord's Supper? How do you experience the presence and power of Christ when you take the bread and the cup? Discuss their responses.

- Read or tell in your own words the information in "Bible Reading and Study." Have participants write responses to the questions in "Reflect." What is your experience of reading and studying the Bible? What benefits do you see in this practice? How might it be challenging? Discuss their responses.

- Read or tell in your own words the information in "Fasting." Have participants write responses to the questions in "Reflect." What is your response to Wesley's ideas about fasting as a spiritual discipline? How might it be challenging for you? How might it be beneficial? Discuss their responses.

What Does the Bible Say?

- Read aloud the opening sentence in "What Does the Bible Say?" Invite participants to read the Bible passages and respond to the instructions in "Reflect on the Bible." Read the following Bible passages. What challenges you or makes you want to know more in the readings? What do they say to you about ways to stay in love with God? Deuteronomy 6:4-9; Matthew 22:34-40; 1 Kings 8; John 4. Discuss their responses. If you have time, you may choose to have the group form three teams. Assign one of the above Bible readings to each team. Have them read their assigned Scripture and discuss it in the team. Share highlights of the team discussions with the entire group.

- Read or tell in your own words the information in the section entitled "Deuteronomy 6:4-9." Invite participants to respond to the questions in "Reflect." What do you love with all your heart, soul, and might? What connections do you see between this love and your love for God? Discuss their responses.

- Read or tell in your own words the information in the section entitled "Matthew 22:34-40." Invite participants to respond to the question in "Reflect." What connections do you see between love for God and love for neighbor? Discuss their responses.

- Read or tell in your own words the information in the section entitled "1 Kings 8." Invite participants to respond to the question in "Reflect." How does worship at your church help you stay in love with God? Discuss their responses.

- Read or tell in your own words the information in the section entitled "John 4." Invite participants to respond to the questions in "Reflect." Is your experience of God's presence different in corporate worship than in other settings? If so, why? What connections do you see in the location of worship and the attitude of worship? Discuss their responses.

CLOSE THE SESSION

- Invite the group to use "Closing – A Guide for Daily Prayer" during the week ahead for their personal prayer. Tell them to read Chapter 6, "Stay in Love With God – Practicing the Rule" and to write responses in the reflection activities.
- Pray aloud the prayer in "Welcoming God's Presence." *Loving God, we seek to love you with all our heart, soul, and might. Make your presence known to us and guide us in our longings. In Christ's name. Amen.*
- Read aloud Psalm 42:1-2 in the section entitled "Scripture."
- Tell participants to write about insights, words, or ideas that come to them as they reflect on Psalm 42:1-2 according to the instructions in "Meditation."
- Invite the group to pray according to the instructions in "Prayer." They may pray aloud or silently. Close the time of prayer by saying aloud "Amen."
- Read aloud John Wesley quote in "Blessing" as a dismissal for the session.

CHAPTER

STAY IN LOVE WITH GOD –
Practicing the Rule

PREPARE AHEAD

Set Up the Learning Area

- Prepare a worship center. Find a small table and cover with an attractive cloth. Place a candle in a candleholder, and place it on the table. Have matches nearby. Place a Bible on the table. Make a poster that lists the three rules: Do No Harm, Do Good, Stay in Love With God. Place this poster where all can see it.
- Prepare a graffiti sheet by writing the words "Stay in Love With God – Practicing the Rule" at the top of a large white sheet of paper or poster board. Put this graffiti sheet in a place such as a wall or a tabletop where participants can easily write on it.

- Arrange chairs in a circle or around a table. Make sure everyone will have a place to sit. Be sensitive to the needs of persons who have disabilities.

Gather Needed Materials

- A copy of *Three Simple Rules for Christian Living* for each participant in the group
- The DVD for *Three Simple Rules for Christian Living*
- This leader guide, in order to have the session plan easily available for your use.
- (Optional) A copy or copies of Rueben Job's book *Three Simple Rules*
- Bibles. If possible, provide several different translations or paraphrases such as the Common English Bible, the New King James Version, the New Revised Standard Version, and *THE MESSAGE*.
- Bible dictionaries and commentaries
- Paper, markers, paper, pencils, nametags
- Whiteboard or newsprint and markers
- Audiovisual equipment: a DVD player and TV for showing the DVD segment for this session

WELCOME THE PARTICIPANTS

Greet the participants as they arrive. Show them the worship center and where additional Bibles and Bible resources are located. Invite them to write or draw on the graffiti sheet "Stay in Love With God – Practicing the Rule" any ideas or images they have about practicing the rule. Tell them to create a nametag and to find a place to sit.

CONSIDER THE QUESTIONS

Invite someone to read aloud the focus question for the rule. How can we put into practice the rule staying in love with God? What difference can our practice make in our own lives and in the lives of others? Invite them to write responses in the space provided in their books. Discuss their responses. Look at the graffiti sheet response. Invite participants to tell about what they have written or drawn.

PRAY TOGETHER

Invite the group to pray aloud the prayer that is printed in their study books: O God of unlimited love, help us in all the demands and challenges of our daily lives to choose and put into action one or more practices that will enable us to stay in love with you. Amen.

VIEW THE DVD SEGMENT

Show the DVD segment for session 6, "Stay in Love With God – Practicing the Rule." Invite participants to respond to the following questions:

1. What are some ways in which our relationship with God is like a marriage relationship? What are some ways in which it is different?
2. When Rueben Job says we should claim our inheritance, what do you think he means? How have you done this in your own life?
3. Job asks the question, "How do we change?" After studying the three simple rules, what are some ways you might try to change?

REFLECT AND RESPOND

What Does the Rule Say?

*   Read or tell in your own words the opening paragraph in this section. Invite participants to respond to the questions in "Reflect

on the Rule." What are your initial ideas about what it means to practice staying in love with God? What has been your experience and understanding of the role of spiritual disciplines in your life? What role do each of the following spiritual disciplines play in your life? Which means most to you? Why? Prayer, Worship and the Lord's Supper, Reading and studying the Bible, Fasting. Discuss their responses.

- Read or tell in your own words the story of Greta's immigration in "The Upper Decks." Invite participants to respond to the questions in "Reflect." What connections do you make with Greta's story? What does this story say to you about God's grace? About practices that will help you to stay in love with God? Discuss their responses.

- Read or tell in your own words the information in "Prayer." Have participants respond to the questions in "Reflect." How has your concept of prayer changed throughout your journey of faith? What experiences have prompted you to practice different forms of prayer? Discuss their responses.

- Read or tell in your own words the information in "Worship and the Lord's Supper." Have participants respond to the questions in "Reflect." How does attending and participating in worship and the Lord's Supper help you experience God's power and presence? How do these practices affect your daily life? How might they affect your life in the future? Discuss their responses.

- Read or tell in your own words the information in "Reading and Studying Scripture." Have participants respond to the questions in "Reflect." How often do you read the Bible? Do you read to gain information or to nurture relationship with God? Which way of reading speaks most to you or nurtures you? Why? Discuss their responses.

- Read or tell in your own words the information in "Fasting." Have participants respond to the questions in "Reflect." What comes to your mind when you consider the practice of fasting? What challenges you about this practice? What benefits do you see in this practice? Do you think that some form of fasting might help you stay in love with God? Why or why not? Discuss their responses.

What Does the Bible Say?

*   Read the opening sentence in this section. Invite participants to read Daniel 1 and 6; Luke 11:1-13; and 1 Corinthians 11:23-26. Have them respond to the questions in "Reflect on the Bible." How do these Scriptures speak to you about the spiritual disciplines of prayer, worship and the Lord's Supper, reading and studying the Bible, and fasting? What do they suggest to you about the importance of spiritual disciplines as a way of staying in love with God? Discuss their responses. If you have time, you may choose to have the group form three teams. Assign one of the above Bible readings to each team. Have them read their assigned Scripture and discuss it in the team. Share highlights of the team discussions with the entire group.

*   Read or tell in your own words the information in the section entitled "Daniel 1 and 6." Have participants respond to the questions in "Reflect." How does Daniel's example affect you as you consider your practice of spiritual disciplines? How has a spiritual discipline served to ground you and hold you steadfast during a difficult time? Discuss their responses.

*   Read or tell in your own words the information in the section entitled "Luke 11:1-13." Have participants respond to the questions in "Reflect." Examine the Lord's Prayer as a pattern for your own prayers. How can you learn to pray by using it as a pattern? In what new ways can it speak to you about God's presence and power and your life of faith? How do you think this prayer can help you stay in love with God? Discuss their responses.

- Read or tell in your own words the information in the section entitled "1 Corinthians 11:23-26." Have participants respond to the questions in "Reflect." What do Paul's words about the significance of the Lord's Supper say to you about the practice of staying in love with God by sharing the Lord's Supper with others? How do you think this practice offers nurture and power for living as a follower of Jesus Christ? How do you think this practice contributes to the unity of the Christian community? Discuss their responses.

Conclusion

Read aloud the paragraph in the section entitled "Conclusion." Invite participants to respond to the questions in "Reflect." After considering the three simple rules, which one seems the most challenging for you at this time of your life? What choices or changes can you make in order to live out the three simple rules for Christian living? Discuss their responses.

CLOSE THE SESSION

- Invite the group to use "Closing – A Guide for Daily Prayer" for their personal prayer. Invite them to work at putting into practice all that they have learned about the three simple rules for Christian living. Ask: What has been most meaningful to you during this study of the three simple rules? Why?
- Pray aloud the prayer in "Welcoming God's Presence." *O God, awaken us to your presence and help us to attend to the practices that keep us in love with you. Keep us mindful of the ways these practices keep us in love with you and with our sisters and brothers as we strive to do no harm and to do good. Amen.*

- Read aloud Psalm 130:5-6 in the section entitled "Scripture."
- Tell participants to write about insights, words, or ideas that come to them as they reflect on the ways we wait for God and enjoy God's companionship according to the instructions in "Meditation."
- Invite the group to pray according to the instructions in "Prayer." They may pray aloud or silently. Close the time of prayer by saying aloud "Amen."
- Read aloud 1 Thessalonians 5:16-18 in "Blessing" as a dismissal for the session.

INTERGENERATIONAL WORSHIP IDEAS

As you study *Three Simple Rules: A Wesleyan Way of Living* by Rueben Job with the children, youth, and adults of your congregation, you may want to plan for group involvement in intergenerational activities. Consider these possibilities:

- Plan a concluding celebration on a Sunday morning that will create a renewed commitment to practicing the three simple rules. Recruit adults, youth, and children to offer testimonies about what they learned and practiced during their study.
- During the study, have the groups learn the song "Stay in Love With God." An intergenerational choir can sing the song during worship.
- Add an intergenerational activity to each session. For example, the combined group might create a group banner for each of the three simple rules. The banners can then be displayed in the sanctuary during worship as a reminder of what the groups have learned.

- Make suggestions of songs or hymns that reflect the three simple rules for those who plan the worship services for the weeks following the study. Have someone name the connections to the three simple rules when the songs are sung.
- Prepare a video or skits that illustrate the three simple rules. Involve actors from all age groups.
- Have children, youth, and adults work together to design the worship altar that reflects the meanings of the three simple rules in the lives of Christians.

A GUIDE FOR DAILY PRAYER

Each session of *Three Simple Rules for Christian Living* ends with
a guide for daily prayer adapted from the guides in Rueben Job's book
Three Simple Rules. Invite participants to continue using them between the
sessions and when the study has been completed. Below you will find an
example of the guide's format.

WELCOMING GOD'S PRESENCE

God of all life, thank you for being with us and for giving us what we
need to live according to your vision for our lives. Guide me as I continue
my efforts to do no harm, to do good, and to stay in love with you. In Christ
I pray. Amen.

SCRIPTURE

Just then a lawyer stood up to test Jesus. "Teacher," he said, "what
must I do to inherit eternal life?" He said to him, "What is written in the

law? What do you read there?" He answered, "You shall love the Lord your God with all your heart, and with all your soul, and with all your strength, and with all your mind; and your neighbor as yourself." And he said to him, "You have given the right answer; do this, and you will live."

—Luke 10:25-28

MEDITATION

Prayerfully reflect on Luke 10:25-28 and how it speaks to you about living according to the three simple rules. Write about your insights from this reflection:

PRAYER

Dear God, thank you for speaking to me through the teachings of Jesus. Help me to live according to his words. In Jesus' name I pray. Amen.

BLESSING

Though we stumble, we shall not fall headlong,
    for the LORD holds us by the hand.

—Psalm 37:24

CPSIA information can be obtained
at www.ICGtesting.com
Printed in the USA
FSHW02n0109061018
52794FS